The Golden Rule: How Income Inequality Will Ruin America

Abstract: There is a high correlation between income inequality and legal inequality in America. As citizens, we should seek to reduce this correlation coefficient because of the disturbing ramifications for the rule of law.

In memory of my father, Ching-Sung Chung a.k.a. "Papi-san"

TABLE OF CONTENTS

I0412793

Introduction

In Disney's <u>Aladdin</u> Jafar states, "You've heard of the golden rule, haven't you? Whoever has the gold makes the rules!" We have all heard this maxim before. The 'golden rule' would be considered positive law or man-made law. The other type of law is categorized as natural law or universal law.

Positive Law is established or recognized by government authority.[1] Natural law is a body of law or a specific principle held to be derived from nature and binding upon human society in the absence of or in addition to positive law.[2]

There is a direct relationship between capitalism and positive law in America. America's laws are continually being shaped by the economy. Unfortunately, America's income inequality is rising. There is a high correlation between income inequality and legal inequality in America. As citizens, we should seek to reduce this correlation coefficient because of the disturbing ramifications for the rule of law.

A. Rule of Law

The American Bar Association[3] ("ABA") has recognized that the definition of the 'rule of law' is based on the belief that the rule of

---

[1] http://www.merriam-webster.com/dictionary/positive%20law
[2] http://www.merriam-webster.com/dictionary/natural+law?show=0&t=1396721248
[3] The American Bar Association is one of the world's largest voluntary professional organizations, with nearly 400,000 members and more than 3,500 entities. It is committed to doing what only a national association of attorneys can do: serving our members, improving the legal profession, eliminating bias and enhancing diversity, and advancing the rule of law throughout the United States

law is a prerequisite for building societies that offer opportunity and equity to all their citizens.[4]

In a similar vein to Joseph Raz's principles in the essay "The Rule of Law and Its Virtue,"[5] written in 1977, the World Justice Project[6] ("WJP") has proposed a working definition of the rule of law that comprises four principles:

1. A system of self-government in which all persons, including the government, are accountable under the law.

2. A system based on fair, publicized, broadly understood and stable laws.

3. A fair, robust, and accessible legal process in which rights and responsibilities based in law are evenly enforced.

4. Diverse, competent, and independent lawyers and judge.[7]

---

and around the world. http://www.americanbar.org/about_the_aba.html
[4]
http://www.americanbar.org/content/dam/aba/migrated/publiced/features/Part1Dia logueROL.authcheckdam.pdf
[5] Joseph Raz's principles include: all laws should be prospective, open, and clear; laws should be stable; the making of laws should be guided, open, clear, and general rules; the independence of the judiciary must be guaranteed; natural justice must be observed; courts must have reviewing power over some principles; courts should be accessible; and the discretion of crime-preventing agencies should not be allowed to pervert the law.
http://www.oxfordscholarship.com/view/10.1093/acprof:oso/9780198253457.001. 0001/acprof-9780198253457-chapter-11
[6] The World Justice Project® (WJP) is an independent, multidisciplinary organization working to advance the rule of law around the world. The rule of law provides the foundation for communities of opportunity and equity – communities that offer sustainable economic development, accountable government, and respect for fundamental rights. http://worldjusticeproject.org/who-we-are
[7] http://worldjusticeproject.org/what-rule-law

The WJP states:

> Establishing the rule of law is fundamental to achieving communities of opportunity and equity—communities that offer sustainable economic development, accountable government, and respect for fundamental rights. Without the rule of law, medicines do not reach health facilities due to corruption; women in rural areas remain unaware of their rights; people are killed in criminal violence; and firms' costs increase because of expropriation risk. The rule of law is the cornerstone to improving public health, safeguarding participation, ensuring security, and fighting poverty.[8]

WJP's Rule of Law Index 2010 Report[9] analyzes 10 dimensions of the rule of law and offers a detailed and comprehensive picture of the extent to which 35 countries around the world adhere to the rule of law:

---

[8]

http://worldjusticeproject.org/sites/default/files/WJP_Rule_of_Law_Index_2010_Report.pdf

[9] The World Justice Project's Rule of Law Index is a quantitative assessment tool designed to offer a detailed and comprehensive picture of the extent to which 35 countries around the world adhere to the rule of law.
http://worldjusticeproject.org/publication/rule-law-index-reports/rule-law-index-2010-report

U.S. Ranking:	U.S./Global	U.S./Peer
• Limited government powers	9/35	7/7
• Absence of corruption	10/35	7/7
• Clear, publicized and stable laws	9/35	6/7
• Order and security	11/35	6/7
• Fundamental rights	11/35	7/7
• Open government	3/35	3/7
• Regulatory enforcement	8/35	5/7
• Access to civil justice	11/35	7/7
• Effective criminal justice	7/35	5/7
• Informal justice	N/A	N/A

The United States' peers are considered countries in Western Europe and North America. The United States' peers are Austria, Canada, France, Netherlands, Spain, and Sweden. WJP's Rule of Law Index 2010 Report states:

> Countries in Western Europe and North America tend to outperform most other countries in all dimensions. These countries are characterized by low levels of corruption, with open and accountable governments, and effective criminal justice systems. In most dimensions, countries in Western Europe obtain higher scores than the United States. For example, Sweden, the Netherlands, Austria, and France receive among the best marks in terms of absence of corruption and access to civil justice. In contrast, most countries in Western Europe do not do as well as the United States and Canada with regard to providing opportunities for the public to voice their concerns and participate in the law making process.

The greatest weakness in Western Europe and North America appears to be related to the accessibility of the civil justice system. In the area of access to legal counsel, for instance, the United States ranks 20th, while Sweden ranks 17th. These are areas that require attention from both policy makers and civil society to ensure that all people, including marginalized groups, are able to benefit from the civil justice system. [10]

As a U.S. citizen, it should be concerning that the United States ranks last in its peer group in regards to "limited government powers," "absence of corruption," "fundamental rights," and "access to justice." It should be alarming that America ranks sixth (out of seventh in its peer group) in "order and security" as well as "clear, publicized, and stable laws." Furthermore, it should be troubling that the U.S. ranks in the bottom half of its peer group in "effective criminal justice and regulatory enforcement."

B. A Case Study

In "Positivism and Normative Inference: Two Key Legal Problems of Late Modernity,"[11] Dr. Eric Engle analyzes the Critical Legal Studies philosophy and Professor Duncan Kennedy's reasoning for this philosophy.[12] Dr. Engle believes that there are

---

[10] *Id.*

[11] http://ssrn.com/abstract=1268520

[12] Proponents of this theory believe that logic and structure attributed to the law

inherent subjective principles that prevent the critical legal studies concepts from being demonstrable. Dr. Engle argues that law cannot truly be called a "science" because he believes it is impossible to apply the law universally, with scientific certainty, or without bias.

Dr. Engle states:

> 'Character evidence' is the most obvious example [of pre-scientific law] where we convict and punish not on the base of scientific certainty but due to the character (whatever that is) of the plaintiff and defendant. Here, let me put in black and white terms lest I am unclear: 'Character evidence' is just a fancy way to say: Niggers in jails, white men in suits go free. If you are going to be pre-scientific you might as well go all the way and make ad hominem arguments and arguments to authority. There is a place for passion in science.

On June 15, 2013, Ethan Couch killed four pedestrians and injured two others in Westlake, Texas.[13] Mr. Couch killed Breanna Mitchell, whose car broke down; Hollie and Shelby Boyles, who

---

grow out of the power relationships of the society. The law exists to support the interests of the party or class that forms it and is merely a collection of beliefs and prejudices that legitimize the injustices of society. The wealthy and the powerful use the law as an instrument for oppression in order to maintain their place in hierarchy. The basic idea of CLS is that the law is politics and it is not neutral or value free. http://www.law.cornell.edu/wex/critical_legal_theory

[13] Mitchell, Mitch. "Teen sentenced to 10 years probation, rehab in 4 deaths". *Fort Worth Star-Telegram*. Retrieved 15 December 2013.

came to assist Breanna; and Brian Jennings, a youth minister who also stopped to help. In addition, Mr. Couch critically injured two of his passengers, Solimon Mohmand and Sergio Molina.[14] The sixteen year-old teen admitted to speeding and being drunk when he lost control of his pickup. Tests revealed he had a blood-alcohol level three times the legal limit and traces of Valium in his system at the time of the accident.[15]

On December 10, 2013, Eric Boyles, the man who lost his wife Hallie and only daughter Shelby in the fatal accident, discovered that Mr. Couch would serve the minimal time in prison for his actions.[16] In fact, Mr. Couch was sentenced to exactly zero days in prison. Although Mr. Couch was driving 70 mph in a 40 mph zone, had a blood alcohol level of 0.24, and had valium in his system Judge Jean Boyd granted Mr. Couch extreme leniency.[17] In lieu of prison time, the Judge sentenced Mr. Couch to ten years of probation and treatment.[18]

---

[14] Solimon had numerous broken bones and internal injuries. Sergio remains paralyzed and communicates by blinking his eyes.

[15] *Id.* (http://www.star-telegram.com/2013/12/10/5408563/teen-sentenced-to-10-years-probation.html?rh=1#storylink=cpy)

[16] http://www.nbcdfw.com/news/local/Judge-Jean-Boyd-Becomes-Target-of-Ethan-Couch-Affluenza-Case-Criticism-235718611.html

[17] http://abcnews.go.com/US/affluenza-dui-case-victims-families-im/story?id=21220171

In assessing the ruling, a New York Times Article suggests the defense of "affluenza" played a critical role in the decision. The Article stated:

> Judge Boyd did not discuss her reasoning for her order, but it came after a psychologist called by the defense argued that Mr. Couch should not be sent to prison because he suffered from 'affluenza' — a term that dates at least to the 1980s to describe the psychological problems that can afflict children of privilege. Prosecutors said they had never heard of a case where the defense tried to blame a young man's conduct on the parents' wealth. And the use of the term and the judge's sentence have outraged the families of those Mr. Couch killed and injured, as well as victim rights advocates who questioned whether a teenager from a low-income family would have received as lenient a penalty.[19]

"This has been a very frustrating experience for me," said prosecutor Richard Alpert. "I'm used to a system where the victims have a voice and their needs are strongly considered. The way the system down here is currently handled, the way the law is, almost all the focus is on the offender."[20]

---

[18] http://www.nbcdfw.com/news/local/Teen-in-Drunken-Crash-That-Killed-Four-Sentenced-to-Probation-235308141.html

[19] http://www.nytimes.com/2013/12/14/us/teenagers-sentence-in-fatal-drunken-driving-case-stirs-affluenza-debate.html?_r=1&

[20] http://www.cnn.com/2014/02/05/us/texas-affluenza-teen/

In the previously referenced, "Positivism and Normative Inference: Two Key Legal Problems of Late Modernity," Dr. Eric Engle contends:

> The system of production (the base or infrastructure) directly influences and even determines the super-structural justifications of the system. That duality – the forces of production (base) and the relations of production (superstructure) – is just basic Marxism. The fact that the mode of production definitely alters the way we think about law can also be seen in the rise and fall of the legal realists . . .[21] All along the way we can trace the development of "realist" thought and their successors by measuring America's rise as an industrial power, decline due to world depression, and re-ascendance as global empire. One can project where the current decline of American power will either lead to a definitive breakdown or to a quasi-fascist rationalization of relations of power – likely, both. *The impetus is nothing other than economics.*[22] [emphasis added]

The relationship between the rule of law and democratic institutions is governed by economics. The systematic danger of economics' influence on the rule of law lies in economic inequality.

---

[21] In agreement with Bentham and against Blackstone the group of legal writers called American legal realists maintain that judges do in fact make law. But against Bentham they maintain that judges should take a hand in making law, and against both Bentham and Blackstone they maintain that judges must be makers of law-and by "must" is meant that judges necessarily make law, that this is intrinsic to the very process or activity of judging. THEODORE M. BENDITT, Law as Rule and Principle, The Harvester Press (1978) p. 1 .
[22] http://ssrn.com/abstract=1268520

C. Law in America

In Mr. Greenwald's book "With Liberty and Justice for Some,"
he describes the rationale for American jurisprudence. He states:

> We are, in the words of John Adams, 'a nations of
> laws, not men.' For Adams, either the law is
> supreme in all cases, or the arbitrary will of rulers
> is. Adams and the other founders viewed the
> preeminence of law over individuals – all
> individuals – as the only protection against the
> tyranny that American colonists had launched a
> revolution to abolish. For that reason, American
> political liberty was always inextricably bound to
> the notion that law reign supreme. . . . A principal
> grievance against King George III was his
> unilateral power to vest in himself and those he
> favored the right to act outside of the law. *The
> goal of the American Revolution was to replace
> this arbitrary will of the monarch with unbending
> equal application of law to everyone* (emphasis
> added).[23]

In Thomas Paine's 1776 pamphlet "Common Sense," he
states:

> Let a crown be placed theron, by which the world
> may know, that so far as we approve of monarchy,
> that in America the Law is King. For as in absolute
> governments the King is law, so in free countries
> the law ought to be King; and there ought to be no
> other.[24]

---

[23] "With Liberty and Justice for Some," by Glenn Greenwald. Location 47/4448 e-book.

[24] http://www.ushistory.org/paine/commonsense/singlehtml.htm

In Thomas Jefferson's 1786 "Answer to Monsieur de Meusnier's Questions," he argues that "the poorest laborer stood on equal ground with the wealthiest millionaire, and generally on a more favored on whenever their rights seem to jar."[25] In Ben Franklin's 1774 "Emblematical Representations," he predicts that an uneven application of laws will create two tiers: the "favored" and the "oppressed." Ben Franklin warns:

> The ordaining of laws in favor of one part of the nation, to the prejudice and oppression of another, is certainly the most erroneous and mistaken policy. An equal dispensation of protection, rights, privileges, and advantages, is what every part is entitled to, and ought to enjoy. . . . These measures never fail to create great and violent jealousies and animosities between the people favored and the people oppressed; whence a total separation of affections, interests, political obligations, and all manner of connections necessarily ensue, by which the whole state is weakened.[26]

The Organization for Security and Co-operation in Europe ("OSCE") describes the rule of law as a cornerstone of its human

---

[25] "In America, no other distinction between man and man had ever been known but that of persons in office exercising powers by authority of the laws, and private individuals. Among these last, the poorest laborer stood on equal ground with the wealthiest millionaire, and generally on a more favored one whenever their rights seem to jar." --Thomas Jefferson: Answers to de Meusnier Questions, 1786. ME 17:8. http://faculty.cua.edu/pennington/Law508/JeffersonRights.htm

[26] Benjamin Franklin, "Emblematical Representations" ca. 1774. https://www.gilderlehrman.org/sites/default/files/inline-pdfs/Founding%20Fathers%20Quotations%20Handout.pdf

rights and democratization activities. "It not only describes formal legal frameworks, but also aims at justice based on the full acceptance of human dignity."[27] When economics disproportionately influence who is accountable under the law, disrupt the administration and enforcement of the law, and create interested judges the rule of law is adversely affected. When the rule of law is adversely affected, democratic institutions like the United States are directly compromised. Economic inequality results in legal inequality.

D. Capitalism's Economic Effect on America

In December 2011, the Organisation for Economic Co-operation and Development[28] ("OECD") released a report which ranked the United States the fourth worst country (out of thirty-four member countries in the OECD) in income inequality level.[29]

The OECD report revealed that the share of national income of the top 1% more than doubled between 1980 and 2008. The richest

[27] http://www.osce.org/what/rule-of-law
[28] The mission of the Organisation for Economic Co-operation and Development (OECD) is to promote policies that will improve the economic and social well-being of people around the world. The OECD was found in 1961 and has 34 member countries.
[29] Rankings: #1-Chile, #2-Mexico, #3-Turkey, #4-United States.
http://www.oecd.org/unitedstates/49170253.pdf

1% now captured 18% of national income compared to 8% in 1980. Meanwhile, the marginal income tax rate has dropped from 70% in 1981 to 35% in 2010. The top 1% of America now collects an average around $1.3 million of after-income while the bottom 20% of America earns on average $17,700 annually.[30]

According to statistics from University of California Santa Cruz Sociology Professor G. William Domhoff, the top 1% of America owns 34.6% of the wealth in total net worth and 42.7% in financial wealth.[31]

According to the Center on Budget and Policy Priorities, the gaps in after-tax income between the top 1% and the middle and poorest fifths of the country more than tripled between 1979 and 2007.[32] In citing statistics released by the Congressional Budget Office ("CBO"), the Center on Budget and Policy Priorities states that there is now greater income concentration at the top of the income scale than at any time since 1928.[33] The United States'

---

[30] *Id.*
[31] http://www2.ucsc.edu/whorulesamerica/power/wealth.html
[32] http://www.cbpp.org/files/6-25-10inc.pdf
[33] *Id.*

current economic period is reminiscent of the Gilded Age of the 1800's.[34]

In his book "Capital in the Twenty-First Century," Thomas Piketty, a professor at the Paris School of Economics, contends that worsening inequality is an inevitable outcome of free-market capitalism. Mr. Piketty suggests that the rise in inequality simply proves markets are working precisely as they should. He argues capitalism's inherent dynamic creates strong forces that disrupt, undermine, and threaten democratic societies.[35]

In Steven Pearlstein's Washington Post Review of Mr. Piketty's book, he explains

Mr. Piketty's position:

> Piketty's prediction of a 21st century of slow growth and extreme inequality is based on historic data and a simple equation. The data, which he assembled with various collaborators in several countries, show that over long periods of time, output per person — productivity — tends to grow at an average of 1 to 1.5 percent. The data also show that average return on investment over long

---

[34] The Gilded Age is a term coined by Mark Twain and Charles Dudley Warner in their 1873 novel, "The Gilded Age: A Tale of Today." Although 1870-1900 marked an era of economic growth in the United States, this period also marked an era of mass unemployment and poverty for U.S. citizens and immigrants in America.
[35] http://www.nytimes.com/2014/01/29/opinion/capitalism-vs-democracy.html?_r=1

periods of time ranges between 4 and 5 percent. . . . Whenever the return on financial capital (investment) is higher than the return on human capital (productivity) for an extended period, it is a matter of simple arithmetic that growing inequality will result. The reason: Those with the highest incomes will save and invest, generating capital income that will allow them to pull away from those relying solely on wages and salaries. It takes only a few generations before this accumulating and accumulated wealth becomes a dominant factor in the economy and the social and political structure.

Indeed, Piketty says, the data show that it has already happened in the United States, where inequality in the distribution of both wealth and income surpasses that of class-bound Europe of 1900. Part of that American story, Piketty writes, reflects the surge in pay for corporate executives and Wall Sreet financiers who make up a large part of the top 1 percent of income earners. As Piketty sees it, *their soaring compensation cannot be adequately explained simply by superior education or performance, but also reflects imperfectly competitive labor and product markets that allow the top 1 percent to extract way more than their real economic contribution.* [36] [emphasis added]

In his article "The Quiet Coup" Simon Johnson, former chief economist to the International Monetary Fund, compares America's bankers to emerging-market oligarchs. Mr. Johnson describes how

---

[36] http://www.washingtonpost.com/opinions/capital-in-the-twenty-first-century-by-thomas-piketty/2014/03/28/ea75727a-a87a-11e3-8599-ce7295b6851c_story.html

U.S. financiers have diverted national resources, notably the trillion dollar bailout, to themselves. While detailing how the U.S. finance industry has pulled off a "quiet coup," he notes:

> From 1973 to 1985, the financial sector never earned more than 16 percent of domestic corporate profits. In 1986, that figure reached 19 percent. In the 1990s, it oscillated between 21 percent and 30 percent, higher than it had ever been in the postwar period. This decade, it reached 41 percent. Pay rose just as dramatically. From 1948 to 1982, average compensation in the financial sector ranged between 99 percent and 108 percent of the average for all domestic private industries. From 1983, it shot upward, reaching 181 percent in 2007. [37]

Mr. Johnson attributes the financial sector's growth and power (as well as the worsening income inequality) to political influence, deregulatory policies, and financial innovation.

The financial industry now accounts for 41% of corporate profits, which in many economists' view is much more than its real economic contribution to business.

In Chrystia Freeland's book "Plutocrats: The Rise of the New Global Super-Rich and Fall of Everyone Else," she identifies the fundamental drivers for worsening income inequality. Globalization,

---

[37] http://www.theatlantic.com/magazine/archive/2009/05/the-quiet-coup/307364/?single_page=true

the technology revolution, and politics are her three main causes for this widening division. Ms. Freeland states:

> These three transformations—the technology revolution, globalization, and the rise of the Washington Consensus—have coincided with an age of strong global economic growth, and also with the reemergence of the plutocrats, this time on a global scale. Among students of income inequality, there is a fierce debate about which of the three is the most important driver of the rise of the 1 percent. Ideology helps to shape the argument. If you are a true-faith believer in the Washington Consensus, you tend to believe rising income inequality is the product of impersonal— and largely benign—economic forces, like the technology revolution and globalization. If you are a liberal and regret the passing of the Treaty of Detroit, you tend to attribute the changed income distribution chiefly to politics. . .[38]
>
> This is an important argument, with real political implications. But, viewed from the summit of the plutocracy, both sides are right. Globalization and the technology revolution have allowed the 1 percent to prosper; but as the plutocrats have been getting richer and more powerful, the collapse of the Treaty of Detroit has meant we have taxed and regulated them less. *It is a return to the first gilded age not only because we are living through an economic revolution, but also because the rules of the game again favor those who are winning it.*[39] [emphasis added]

---

[38] *Id.* (Kindle Locations 431-437).
[39] *Id.* (Kindle Locations 437-441).

In his lecture "Growth and Interaction in the World Economy – The Roots of Modernity,"[40] Angus Maddison, a notable economist, outlines the tremendous economic growth period we are currently experiencing. Between 1820 and 1998, there has been an unprecedented rise[41] in economic prosperity as a result of the industrial revolution. Just as the industrial revolution delineated "the Haves" and "Have Nots," the New Gilded Age we are currently experiencing is further separating the few from the masses, but on an even grander scale.

Scale is one reason for the magnified difference in earning. In the past, an opera singer's live performance could only reach a limited amount of human ears. Now there is radio, television, and internet to capture a larger *global* audience (for both live performances and

---

40

http://www.ggdc.net/maddison/other_books/Growth_and_Interaction_in_the_Wor ld_Economy.pdf

[41] "In the period between AD 1 and 1000, the GDP of western Europe on average actually shrank at an annual compounded rate of 0.01 percent. People in 1000 were, on average , a little poorer than they had been a thousand years before. In the Western offshoots the economy grew by 0.05 percent. Between 1000 and 1820— more than eight centuries— the average annual compounded growth was 0.34 percent in western Europe and 0.35 percent in the Western offshoots. Then the world changed utterly. The economy took off—between 1820 and 1998 in western Europe it grew at an average annual rate of 2.13 percent, and in the Western offshoots it surged at an average annual rate of 3.68 percent." Freeland, Chrystia (2012-10-11). Plutocrats: The Rise of the New Global Super-Rich and the Fall of Everyone Else (Kindle Locations 282-287). Penguin Group US. Kindle Edition.

delayed viewings) and thus more revenue. An author who was once limited to manual copying can now wholeheartedly tap into the world's connectedness through e-books, audio books, prints in multiple languages, movie deals, and laser printing. The effects of technology and globalization are no mystery. In his article entitled "The Economics of Superstars," Sherwin Rosen, an economist from the University of Chicago, argued that technological changes would allow the best performers in a given field to serve a bigger market and thus reap a greater share of its revenue. But this would also reduce the spoils available to the less gifted in the business.[42] This is known as the Rosen Effect.

Over a century ago, Alfred Marshall, a neoclassical economist, noticed that purveyors of luxury stood to disproportionately gain as the rich became richer. "Those who work for the super-rich can charge super-fees."[43] Even those players who do not participate directly in globalization may benefit from it. Interior designers, artists, musicians, and even lawyers in high-demand may profit

---

[42]

http://www.nytimes.com/2010/12/26/business/26excerpt.html?pagewanted=all&_r=0

[43] http://www.theglobeandmail.com/report-on-business/rob-magazine/how-to-become-a-plutocrat/article4573020/

handsomely as their clients become uber-wealthy. This 'rising-tide' observation is known as the Marshall Effect.

In 1907, Lida F. Baldwin quoted an article from the August 1870 issue of The Atlantic Monthly: "We hear now on all sides the term 'Robber Barons' applied to some of the great capitalists. . . . The old robber barons of the Middle Ages who plundered sword in hand and lance in rest were more honest than this new aristocracy of swindling millionaires."[44] Ms. Baldwin was complaining of how little had changed in the past 35 years.

E. Capitalism's Political Influence on America

In the previously mentioned article "The Quiet Coup," Mr. Johnson warns "of the two-way money-and-power corridor now running between Washington and the modern oligarchs Wall Street." In comparing the U.S. to a banana republic, he writes:

> In its depth and suddenness, the U.S. economic and financial crisis is shockingly reminiscent of moments we have recently seen in emerging markets. . . Just as in emerging-market crises, the weakness in the banking system has quickly rippled out into the rest of the economy, causing a severe economic contraction and hardship for

---

[44] http://en.wikipedia.org/wiki/Robber_baron_%28industrialist%29 quoting http://books.google.com/books?id=B2wAAAAAYAAJ&pg=PA683#v=onepage&q&f=false

millions of people. But there's a deeper and more disturbing similarity: Elite business interests—financiers, in the case of the U.S.—played a central role in creating the crisis, making ever-larger gambles, with the implicit backing of the government, until the inevitable collapse. More alarming, they are now using their influence to prevent precisely the sorts of reforms that are needed, and fast, to pull the economy out of its nosedive. The government seems helpless, or unwilling, to act against them. . . . The great wealth that the financial sector created and concentrated gave bankers enormous political weight—a weight not seen in the U.S. since the era of J.P. Morgan (the man). But that first age of banking oligarchs came to an end with the passage of significant banking regulation in response to the Great Depression; the reemergence of an American financial oligarchy is quite recent. [45]

In his 1994 Atlantic Monthly article "The Age of Social Transformation," Peter Drucker explains, "Marx's great insight was that the factory worker does not and cannot own the tools of production, and therefore is 'alienated.' There was no way, Marx pointed out, for the worker to own the steam engine and to be able to take it with him when moving from one job to another. The capitalist had to own the steam engine and control it." This was the primary

[45] http://www.theatlantic.com/magazine/archive/2009/05/the-quiet-coup/307364/?single_page=true

power and the root cause for Ms. Baldwin's 'robber barons' complaint.

In describing the rise of financiers, Ms. Freeman notes:

> Instead of working for the owners of capital—whether they are industrial magnates or the shareholders of publicly traded companies—financiers have discovered they can themselves own the capital and, with it, the companies. . . . Of the forty thousand Americans with investable assets of more than $30 million, a group described by Merrill Lynch, which produces the premier annual study of the wealthy, as "ultra high net worth individuals," 40 percent were in finance. . . . Wall Street significantly outearned Main Street. Collectively, the executives at publicly traded Wall Street firms earned more than the executives of nonfinancial companies. Wall Street investors, such as hedge fund managers or private equity chiefs, did even better. "In 2004," Kaplan and Rauh write, "nine times as many Wall Street investors earned in excess of $ 100 million as public company CEOs. *In fact, the top twenty-five hedge fund managers combined appeared to have earned more than all five hundred S&P 500 CEOs combined.*"[46] [emphasis added]

In America, today's perceived capitalism has been hi-jacked by the financial elites' pro-business agenda. In his article "Capitalism

---

[46] Freeland, Chrystia (2012-10-11). Plutocrats: The Rise of the New Global Super-Rich and the Fall of Everyone Else (Kindle Locations 2093-2106). Penguin Group US. Kindle Edition.

after the Crisis," Luigi Zingales, a professor at the University of Chicago Booth School of Business, writes:

> True capitalism lacks a strong lobby. That assertion might appear strange in light of the billions of dollars firms spend lobbying Congress in America, but that is exactly the point. Most lobbying seeks to tilt the playing field in one direction or another, not to level it. Most lobbying is pro-business, in the sense that it promotes the interests of existing businesses, not pro-market in the sense of fostering truly free and open competition. Open competition forces established firms to prove their competence again and again; strong successful market players therefore often use their muscle to restrict such competition, and to strengthen their positions. As a result, serious tensions emerge between a pro-market agenda and a pro-business one."[47]

Over 100 years ago, we referred to businessmen who used what were considered to be exploitative practices to amass their wealth as "robber barons." The systematic inequality of the original Gilded Age has returned.[48] The main difference today is the "robber barons" are hedge-fund managers and financiers instead of oil magnates and railroad titans. Like the saying goes, "history doesn't repeat itself but it often rhymes."[49]

---

[47] http://nationalaffairs.com/publications/detail/capitalism-after-the-crisis
[48] The Pew Research Center has indicated that U.S. income inequality is the highest it's been since 1928. http://www.pewresearch.org/fact-tank/2014/01/07/5-facts-about-economic-inequality/

In Timothy Noah's book "The Great Divergence," he states:

> All my life I've heard Latin America described as a failed society (or collection of failed societies) because of its grotesque maldistribution of wealth. Peasants in rags beg for food outside the high walls of opulent villas, and so on. But according to the Central Intelligence Agency (whose patriotism I hesitate to question), income distribution in the United States is more unequal than in Guyana, Nicaragua, and Venezuela, and roughly on par with Uruguay, Argentina, and Ecuador. Income inequality is actually declining in Latin America even as it continues to increase in the United States. *Economically speaking, the richest nation on earth is starting to resemble a banana republic.*[50] [emphasis added]

In Nick Kristoff's New York Times article "Our Banana Republic," he notes:

> In my reporting, I regularly travel to banana republics notorious for their inequality. In some of these plutocracies, the richest 1 percent of the population gobbles up 20 percent of the national pie. But guess what? You no longer need to travel to distant and dangerous countries to observe such rapacious inequality. We now have it right here at home. . . . *The richest 1 percent of Americans now take home almost 24 percent of income, up from almost 9 percent in 1976.*[51] [emphasis added]

---

[49] http://quoteinvestigator.com/2014/01/12/history-rhymes/
[50] http://img.slate.com/media/3/100914_NoahT_GreatDivergence.pdf
[51]

http://www.nytimes.com/2010/11/07/opinion/07kristof.html?partner=rss&emc=rss&_r=0

Banana republics represent disturbing distributions of income, influence, power, and quality of life. America's government is increasingly displaying signs of power by a small dominant class (oligarchy), and influence by the wealthy (plutocracy).

In his academic article "Economic Inequality and Political Representation," Larry Bartels, a political scientist at Princeton, notes, "In almost every instance, senators appear to be considerably more responsive to the opinions of affluent constituents than to the opinions of middle-class constituents, while the opinions of constituents in the bottom third of the income distribution have no apparent statistical effect on their senators' roll call votes."[52] It is no coincidence that more than half the members of the Congress are now millionaires.[53] The financial elite have diligently created an environment of cognitive state capture and systemic capture in our political system.

---

[52] http://www.princeton.edu/~bartels/economic.pdf
[53] http://www.nytimes.com/2014/01/10/us/politics/more-than-half-the-members-of-congress-are-millionaires-analysis-finds.html?_r=0

F. America's Two-Tiered Legal System

During an interview at Meet the Press in 2010, Alan Greenspan, former Federal Reserve Chairman, answered questions regarding his view of the recession and recovery. Mr. Greenspan stated:

> I think we're in a pause in a recovery, a modest recovery. But a pause in the modest recovery feels like quasi-recession. Our problem, basically, is that we have a very distorted economy in the sense that there has been a significant recovery in a limited area of the economy amongst high-income individuals who have just had $800 billion added to their 401(k)s and are spending it and are carrying what consumption there is. Large banks, who are doing much better, and large corporations, whom you point out and the–and everyone's pointing out, are in excellent shape. The rest of the economy, small business, small banks, and a very significant amount of the labor force, which is in tragic unemployment, long-term unemployment, that is pulling the economy apart. The average of those two is what we are looking at, *but they are fundamentally two separate types of economy.* [54] [emphasis added]

The two separate types of economy Mr. Greenspan identifies have created a two-tiered legal system in America. During a financial-crisis hearing before Congress in 2008, Mr. Greenspan was

---

[54] www.msnbc.msn.com/id/38487969/ns/meet_the_press-transcripts/t/meet-press-transcript-august/#.UKt4EYWs0w4

asked about the error in his ideology for lack of government regulations and self-policing of the financial markets. He testified:

> Well, remember that what an ideology is, is a conceptual framework with the way people deal with reality. Everyone has one. You have to -- to exist, you need an ideology. The question is whether it is accurate or not. And what I'm saying to you is, yes, I've found a flaw. . . . in the model that I perceived as the critical functioning structure that defines how the world works. . . That's precisely the reason I was shocked, because I had been going for 40 years or more with very considerable evidence that it was working exceptionally well.[55]

For 40 years, Mr. Greenspan believed the financial markets could self-regulate. He has since admitted a flaw in his philosophy and no longer believes this ideology to be accurate. Many citizens of the United States have yet to realize the flaw in their model, which they perceive as the critical functioning structure of how America works. America has been built upon the premise that it is a land of equal opportunity. However, study after study is revealing statistics that directly counter this belief.

---

[55] http://www.pbs.org/newshour/bb/business-july-dec08-crisishearing_10-23/

Aziz Rana, a professor at Cornell Law School and author of "The Two Faces of American Freedom," describes the ideal of equal opportunity as a false promise.

Mr. Rana writes:

> Despite various tax cuts over the past 30 years, not only have income and wealth inequality dramatically increased, but the ability of individuals to rise out of their own class has declined. Social stagnation is increasingly the norm, with poverty rates the highest in 15 years, real wage gains worse even than during the decade of the Great Depression, average earnings barely above what they were 50 years ago, and more than 80 percent of the income growth of the past 25 years going to the top 1 percent. In fact, since 1983, the bottom 40 percent of households have seen real *declines* in their income and the same goes for the bottom 60 percent when it comes to wealth. We know what the economic status quo does: It redistributes upwards.[56]

In 2007, the Brookings Institution released a report that states:

- Contrary to American beliefs about equality of opportunity, a child's economic position is heavily influenced by that of his or her parents.
- 42% of children born to parents in the bottom fifth of the income distribution remain in the bottom.
- 6 percent of children born to parents with family income at the very bottom move to the very top. [57]

---

[56] http://www.salon.com/2012/02/12/americas_failed_promise_of_equal_opportunity/

[57] http://www.brookings.edu/research/papers/2007/11/generations-isaacs

The Gini coefficient is the most common benchmark formula to assess the equality of a country. This index measures the degree of inequality in the distribution of family income in a country.[58] A Gini coefficient of zero means perfect equality. A Gini coefficient of one represents maximum inequality.

Bo Xilai, a former politician of Chongqing, China and critic of China's rising inequality, once warned,[59] "If only a few people are rich, then we'll slide into capitalism. We've failed. If a new capitalist class is created then we'll really have turned into a wrong road." [60] He made this statement in response to data that revealed China's Gini coefficient had surpassed 0.46. [61] The United States' Gini coefficient is .45 (2007).[62]

As Joseph E. Stiglitz, a Nobel laureate in economics, former chairman of the Council of Economic Advisers, and chief economist

[58] https://www.cia.gov/library/publications/the-world-factbook/rankorder/2172rank.html
[59] http://www.bloomberg.com/news/2012-04-10/china-s-bo-xilai-ousted-from-top-party-committees-reuters-says.html
[60] http://www.businessweek.com/articles/2012-04-30/mystery-and-rumor-dominate-china-in-the-time-of-bo#p2
[61] http://www.businessweek.com/finance/occupy-wall-street/archives/2011/12/chinas_wealth_disparity_erupts_in_wukan_protests.html
[62] https://www.cia.gov/library/publications/the-world-factbook/rankorder/2172rank.html

for the World Bank, warns, "Americans are coming to realize that their cherished narrative of social and economic mobility is a myth. Grand deceptions of this magnitude are hard to maintain for long — and the country has already been through a couple of decades of self-deception."[63]

As stated by the WJP, the accessibility of America's civil justice system is one if its greatest flaws regarding how the rule of law is administered. Texas cases like Ethan Couch's case represent a grotesque unequal administration of the law. America's administration of the rule of law is certainly not the only reason for inequality. Nevertheless, pervasive access to justice issues, sentencing discrepancies, lobbying influence, and cronyism tendencies are detrimental to America properly functioning as a democratic institution. America's two-tiered system systematically applies legal formalism to low socioeconomic classes, while favoring legal realism when it is advantageous to high socioeconomic classes.

---

[63] http://opinionator.blogs.nytimes.com/2013/02/16/equal-opportunity-our-national-myth/?_php=true&_type=blogs&_r=0

Several years after the financial meltdown that generated hundreds of billions in losses, there still has not been any prosecution of senior executives. In Gretchen Morgenson's New York Times article "In Financial Crisis, No Prosecution of Top Figures," she documents:

> This stands in stark contrast to the failure of many savings and loan institutions in the late 1980s. In the wake of that debacle, special government task forces referred 1,100 cases to prosecutors, resulting in more than 800 bank officials going to jail. Among the best-known: Charles H. Keating Jr., of Lincoln Savings and Loan in Arizona, and David Paul, of Centrust Bank in Florida. . . .

> This is not some evil conspiracy of two guys sitting in a room saying we should let people create crony capitalism and steal with impunity," said William K. Black, a professor of law at University of Missouri, Kansas City, and the federal government's director of litigation during the savings and loan crisis. "But their policies have created an exceptional criminogenic environment. There were no criminal referrals from the regulators. No fraud working groups. No national task force. There has been no effective punishment of the elites here."[64]

64

http://www.nytimes.com/2011/04/14/business/14prosecute.html?adxnnl=1&adxnn lx=1396987566-GjtAa1OWtYhl8m/TaQagbw

Even Mr. Greenspan testified:

> There are two fundamental reforms we need: adequate capital and to get far higher enforcement of fraud statutes – existing ones – I'm not even talking about new ones. *Things were being done which were certainly illegal and clearly criminal in certain cases.* If you cannot trust your counterparties, it [capital markets] won't work. And indeed we saw that it didn't.[65] [emphasis added]

The rule of law in the United States is compromised when it has a disparate impact on low socioeconomic classes;[66] promotes a supposed universal "war on drugs," but administers drug sentences unevenly;[67] requires mandatory minimum sentencing for blue-collar crime, but negotiates monetary settlements for white-collar crime;[68] sentences black men to nearly 20% longer terms than white men for similar crimes; [69] prevents immigrants and indigent citizens from access to justice; [70] and imprisons more of its population than any other country.[71]

---

[65] http://steadfastfinances.com/blog/2010/11/11/greenspan-admits-financial-crisis-was-caused-by-fraud-criminal-actions/

[66] http://www.apa.org/pi/ses/resources/publications/factsheet-education.aspx

[67] http://www.drugpolicy.org/drug-facts/cocaine-and-crack-facts

[68] http://www.salon.com/2009/01/28/prosecutions_3/

[69] http://online.wsj.com/news/articles/SB10001424127887324432004578304463789858002

[70] https://www.aclu.org/blog/human-rights-immigrants-rights/immigrants-have-no-access-justice

G. Conclusion

The OSCE describes the rule of law as a cornerstone of its human rights and democratization activities. The ABA has recognized that the definition of the 'rule of law' is based on the belief that the rule of law is a prerequisite for building societies that offer opportunity and equity to all their citizens. The economic influence of inequality negatively impacts how the rule of law is administered in the United States. Economic inequality begets legal inequality.

America's administration of the rule of law is not meant and should not be used to advance the cause of inequality. Unfortunately, America's income inequality is rising. There is a high correlation between income inequality and legal inequality in America. As citizens, we should seek to reduce this correlation coefficient because of the disturbing ramifications for the rule of law.

---

[71] http://www.economist.com/node/16636027